Even If: A Four-Week Journal about Change -

Published by Orange, a division of The reThin
5870 Charlotte Lane, Suite 300
Cumming, GA 30040 U.S.A.

Other Orange products are available online and direct from the publisher.
Visit our website at www.WhatIsOrange.org for more resources like these.

ISBN: 978-1-63570-176-0

Writing & Editing Team: Leslie Mack, Lauren Sellers, Sarah Anderson, Ashley Strot, Ben Crawshaw
Cover Artwork: Lineage Film Company and Plotwist Creative
Book & Cover Design: Plotwist Creative
Project Management: Brian Sharp

Printed in the United States of America

First Edition 2021
1 2 3 4 5 6 7 8 9 10
Print Date 05/28/2021

Change isn't always easy. We get it.

Like basically everybody, you're probably dealing with change right now. It could be a change in your class schedule, a change in your group of friends, or a change at home or work. Maybe you're a junior, and your best friend is a senior and about to graduate. Maybe your mom is about to get remarried. Maybe your body is changing.

Maybe your mood is changing - even as you read this!

We want you to know that no matter what type of change you're facing, you can count on the One who never changes. When nothing else feels stable, God is. You can trust that God is committed to hearing you, knowing you, loving you, and being with you, even if everything else around you changes.

God is the solid, unmovable ground upon which we can stand.

When we trust God, we can experience peace, even in the midst of crazy change. Even if things don't go the way we want them to. (And even if everything turns out better than expected.)

The truth is, everything changes, but some things never change: God never changes. God is with you. God is bigger than your fear. And God can use change to make you stronger.

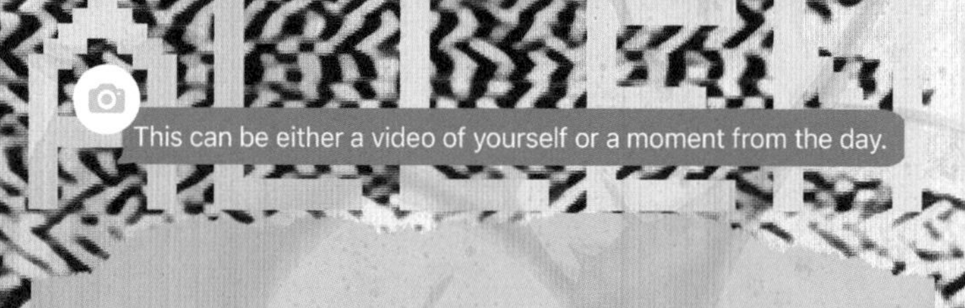

30 DAY PHOTO CHALLENGE

When you go through change, you rarely realize how much you grow until it's over. For the next 30 days, take one photo or one 10-second video every day. This can be a video in yourself or a moment from the day. When you finish this journal, put all of them together in a TikTok or Instagram Reels style video, and save it as a reminder of what God can do in your life in only 30 days.

You can also post using #EvenIfJournal.

PART 1

GOD NEVER CHANGES

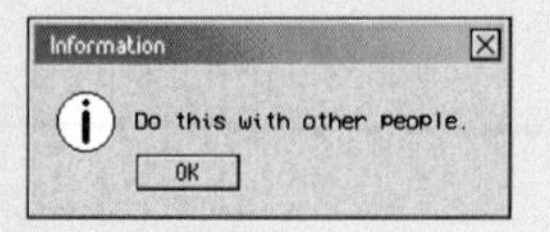

Talk with some friends to identify ways that God never changed, even while that situation was happening. Fill in the spaces below:

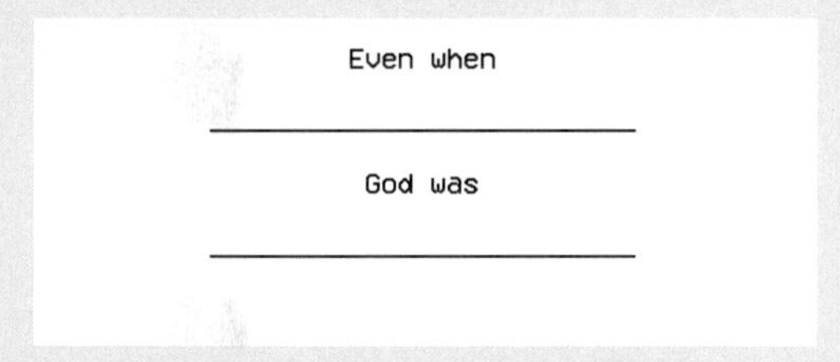

Take a picture of the box above. Share it with your group and include a caption about how God was with you even when life was really uncertain. Then, save it in your phone as a reminder you can use to remember that God is with you, even if...

Say cheese! Don't forget to capture today.

Re-read the experience you just wrote about and write out a prayer in response.

Share with God how you feel about it.

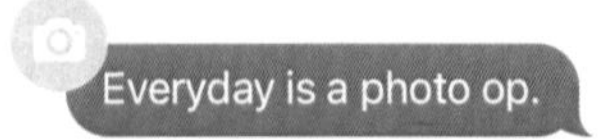

Remember, God doesn't change
even if...

Capture you at this moment.

DAY 1

// Isaiah 40:8 NLT

"The grass withers and the flowers fade, but the word of our God stands forever."

Take a walk outside and look at the nature around you. Whether it's the grass, trees on the street, a neighbor's dog or cat, or something in the sky, nature is all around us and is constantly changing from season to season. Sometimes, this change is noticeable–like when you see leaves change colors during the fall. Other times, it's more gradual–like when an
anthill grows in size over several months. Regardless of whether the change is fast or slow, there's another thing all nature has in common: it will eventually fade. However, in today's verse, we learn that, unlike nature, God's promises never fade.

How can what you see in nature this week be a reminder that God's promises never fade? Spend a little bit of time outside this week. List some of the things you notice that can be reminders of God being present in your life.

____

____

____

____

____

____

____

Say cheese! Don't forget to capture today.

DAY 2

// Psalm 33:11 NLT

"But the Lord's plans stand firm forever;
his intentions can never be shaken."

When plans change at the last minute, it can be incredibly frustrating, and inconsistent. People can make you second guess whether or not they are worthy of your trust. However, you can be assured that God's commitment and intentions to love you don't change. God is trustworthy. The author of Psalm 33 tells us that God is firm, unmovable, and reliable. God's plans for you include never leaving you to do life alone, always hearing you when you call out, and always being found when you seek God with your whole heart.

Reflect on times in the past when trusting God has been difficult. Write down details of the situation and what ultimately ended up happening. Explore what factors made you feel unsure about trusting God at the time, then jot down a one-line prayer you can say out loud in future situations when you find it difficult to trust God.

You look good! You should take a picture or a video!

DAY 3

// 2 Corinthians 4:18b NLT

"For the things we see now will soon be gone,
but the things we cannot see will last forever."

We'll always experience change. Sometimes change will feel like a rollercoaster–it will be obvious and drastic and affect your sense of safety. Other times you might notice the symptoms of change more than the change itself–you feel stressed or your sleeping pattern is off or something just feels weird. We see change happening around us all the time at home, at school, in relationships, in nature, and on sports teams. By contrast, though, the Bible tells us that what we see is fleeting. In fact, God urges us to build our lives around or focus on what we CANNOT see: God and God's commitment to never change.

Take some time to write down two lists: List things that are subject to change and list things that are unchanging, reliable, and consistent in your life.

SUBJECT TO CHANGE	UNCHANGING
______________________	______________________
______________________	______________________
______________________	______________________
______________________	______________________
______________________	______________________
______________________	______________________
______________________	______________________

Everyday is a photo op.

DAY 4

// Psalm 102:12 NLT

"But you, O Lord, will sit on your throne forever.
Your fame will endure to every generation.

Have you ever heard someone older say, "When I was your age..." about how much has changed since they were younger—from cars to TVs to phones? While times certainly have changed over thousands of years (and will continue to change), this verse reminds us God's fame has not, and will not, change. That means God is always bigger than what's happening in the world, and God will always deserve to be at the center of our attention. God will be there for his creation, generation after generation.

Prepare some specific questions to ask adults in your life about how the world around them has changed since they were your age. Then, ask them to tell you about how God has NOT changed in that time, too. Capture any advice they offer about how they learned to handle change.

Capture you at this moment.

DAY 5

// Numbers 23:19a NLT

"God is not a man, so he does not lie. He is not human, so he does not change His mind."

When someone lies to you, much of what you thought about that person usually changes in an instant. Today's verse emphasizes how reliable God is. It reminds us we can always trust in God's unchanging ways. God never lies to us, tricks us, or changes His mind about loving us. The next time you're tempted to bend the truth, look to God's unchanging character as an example of how you should live.

What are some areas in your life where you want to be more consistent? What is one thing you can do today to begin working on your ability to be consistent?

Don't forget to capture a picture or a video clip of yourself today.

// Isaiah 43:2 NLT

"When you go through deep waters, I will be with you. When you go through rivers of difficulty, you will not drown. When you walk through the fire of oppression, you will not be burned up; the flames will not consume you."

This past week at my youth group, we talked about the characteristics of God. My pastor asked us to look at a list of traits we had come up with together the week before and find the word that sticks out to us the most. Mine was the word "gentle." I remembered the times in lockdown when the world felt so out of place, and I was just trying to stay on my feet while everything around me was crumbling. I remembered the first time I sensed God's voice, tenderly in the night when my worries took over, telling me that everything's alright. God's voice gently brings us into God's peace and restores, or calms, our hearts. God pulls us up out of the waters or goes with us into the unknown when we are scared of what lies beneath. We see God working to turn ashes and difficult circumstances into beauty. We can remember that even when the water is too deep, the embers are too bright to see the future, and change feels overwhelming, God never changes. God stays when everyone else walks away; God is here for you no matter what.

How does knowing that God never changes affect how you see change in your own life?

______

______

______

______

______

______

Say cheese! Don't forget to capture today.

DAY 7: MEMORY VERSE

// Hebrews 13:8 NLT

"Jesus Christ is the same yesterday,
today, and forever."

When we memorize Scripture, we're able to recall important truths when we need them most.

1. Try memorizing this verse by repeating the words "yesterday, today, and forever" throughout your day.

2. After a day of just those words, add in the other phrases on day two.

3. Write down the Scripture from memory at breakfast, lunch, and dinner to see what progress you've made.

Capture you at this moment.

PART 2

GOD IS WITH YOU

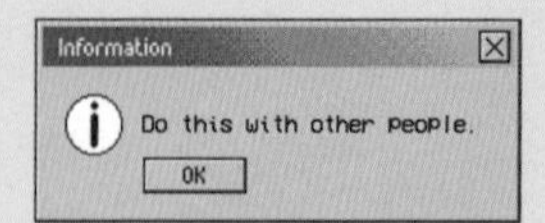

"When you pass through the waters, I will be with you; and when you pass through the rivers, they will not sweep over you. When you walk through the fire, you will not be burned; the flames will not set you ablaze."

Isaiah 43:2 NIV

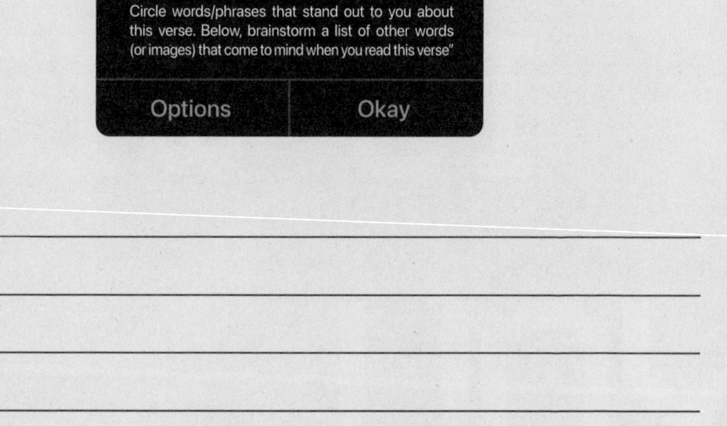

You look good! You should take a picture or a video!

Create a bulleted list of things that MIGHT happen this year - good, neutral, or difficult.

GOOD THINGS	NEITHER GOOD NOR BAD THINGS	DIFFICULT THINGS THAT MIGHT HAPPEN

Say cheese! Don't forget to capture today.

God is with you
even if...

// Psalms 55:22 NLT

**"Give your burdens to the Lord, and he will take care of you.
He will not permit the godly to slip and fall."**

Imagine walking down the street, picking up a small rock, and tossing it into your backpack. Then, as you see more rocks on the sidewalk, you put those in your backpack, too. Now, after walking around for a bit with those rocks, you'd probably begin to realize that what started out as a manageable weight has now become more than you can carry. The same is true with our burden–or the challenges and worries we carry. God has not called us to carry our burdens alone. In fact, He wants you to give Him EVERYTHING that burdens you.

What are you carrying that is weighing you down? List some things here.

How is your life being affected by the burdens you are carrying?

**Write an honest prayer to God about your big and small concerns.
Remember that God wants to take care of you.**

Everyday is a photo op.

DAY 2

// John 14:16-17a NLT

16 "And I will ask the Father, and he will give you another Advocate,[a] who will never leave you."
17 "He is the Holy Spirit, who leads into all truth."

Is there someone in your life who you can always go to for good advice? Maybe it's a parent, teacher, coach, or your Small Group Leader at church. Each of these is someone God has placed in your life to guide you, and they can be especially helpful during difficult times of change. On top of that, Jesus reminds us that God not only gives us people to guide us in life, but He has also sent His Holy Spirit to be an Advocate–or a helper and comforter–along the way. While people in our life will come and go, it's comforting to know God's Spirit will never leave.

Sometimes, it's challenging to see what's true when we are going through change. Think of a change you are facing now or may face in the future. Write a prayer to the Holy Spirit asking for help to see the facts and to guide you as you make decisions. Thank the Holy Spirit for being a helper and a comforter.

Capture you at this moment.

DAY 3

// Psalm 120:1 NLT

"I took my troubles to the Lord; I cried out to him,
and he answered my prayer."

When was the last time you "cried out" about something? Maybe it was last year when you broke up with the person you had been dating. Or maybe it was last week when you stubbed your toe on a chair (it happens). For some, crying out comes easily when they share emotional pain or stress. For others, crying out is more of a response to a physical injury—as opposed to an emotional one. No matter which way you tend to lean, when we go through struggles and seasons of change, the writer of this verse reminds us that crying out to God is always okay. Whatever uncertainties you're facing today, cry out to God in prayer. Share whatever you're going through, and be confident He is listening and is with you.

Journal about the last time you cried out. Here are some questions to help you start: ***When was the last time you outwardly expressed your deepest thoughts and feelings about troubles you were facing? What was happening? Who was there for you? What are some benefits of taking our biggest concerns to God?***

Don't forget to capture a picture or a video clip of yourself today.

DAY 4

// Proverbs 18:10 NIV

10 "The name of the Lord is a fortified tower;
the righteous run to it and are safe."

Have you ever been caught off guard by a thunderstorm? Suddenly, you were inconveniently drenched from head to toe. Sometimes, it can be a frightening experience, especially when lightning is involved. During this time, our first thought is usually to seek shelter—fast! Similarly, in this verse, Solomon reminds us that God wants to be that shelter for us as well. He is our refuge during our personal trials and Someone we can run to when life's unexpected thunderstorms catch us by surprise.

"What are some traits of a strong tower or a "safe place" that come to mind? For example "strong bricks" or "protected by being high off the ground, far from danger" might be some of the images you visualize. In the space below list or draw what comes to mind for you. When you think of God as a strong tower for you, which of his traits give you the most comfort?"

Say cheese! Don't forget to capture today.

DAY 5

// Joshua 1:9b NIV

9 "Have I not commanded you? Be strong and courageous. Do not be afraid; do not be discouraged, for the Lord your God will be with you wherever you go."

Few things make us more afraid than the thought of the unknown—like starting at a new school, moving to a different town, or experiencing a change in friendship or relationship status. While our circumstances could change in an instant, God urges us not to be afraid but to face those moments with courage. Now, God tells us this not because things will always turn out the way we want. Rather, God tells us this because God promises to be by our side the entire time.

Think of a friend who is facing a difficult month or year. In the space below, write a prayer for them or an encouraging note to them. Take a picture of it and send it to them this week letting them know that you are with them—and God is, too.

Capture you at this moment.

// Joshua 1:9 NLT

"This is my command—be strong and courageous! Do not be afraid or discouraged. For the Lord your God is with you wherever you go."

Have you ever been in a season where God flips everything you thought you knew right on its head, and you just didn't know how to feel? That's probably exactly what Joshua, the author of this verse, felt. After the death of Moses, the Israelite nation's leader, the Lord asked Joshua to take over what He had prepared for Moses to do. Joshua became the leader of a whole nation and would be leading them to cross the Jordan River. For Joshua, you can imagine how overwhelming that big of a change could be. God promised Joshua He would provide everything he needed to cross the river and enter the land that would become their home. All He asked was that Joshua trust in Him and not let the situation discourage him. And God does the same for us. All you have to do is trust in His plans. He uses the change you go through to change what is within you! This means changing your heart and how you see things, just as He did for Joshua.

Think of a change that you typically view as negative (getting new teachers every year, for example). What does being strong and courageous look like in your life?

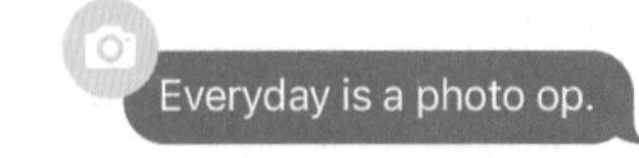

DAY 7: MEMORY VERSE

// John 16:33 NIV

"I have told you these things that in me you may have peace. in this world you will have trouble, but take heart! I have overcome the world."

Memorizing Scripture helps us internalize what we're reading. Sometimes, it's easy to just read the words of Scripture and not really think about the deeper meaning behind them. When you take the time to memorize Scripture, it helps you stop and think about what's actually being communicated in the text.

1. With a dry-erase marker or makeup, write the verse on your mirror so you see it daily when you first wake up.

2. Repeat the verse to yourself a few times each morning, then erase it.

3. At night before going to bed, write the verse on your mirror from memory for the next morning.

____

____

____

____

____

____

____

Capture you at this moment.

PART 3

GOD IS BIGGER THAN YOUR FEARS

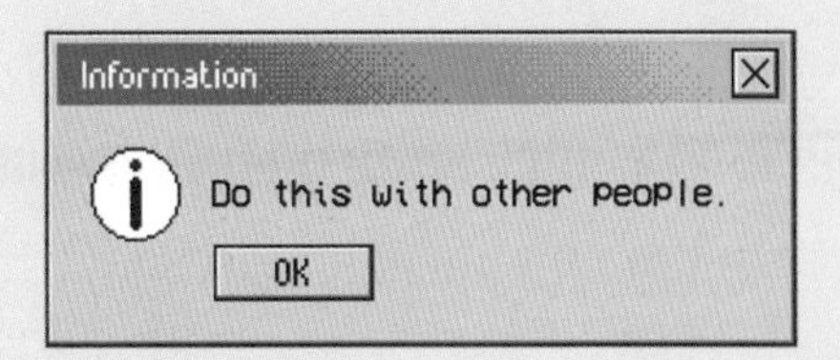

How does change make you feel?

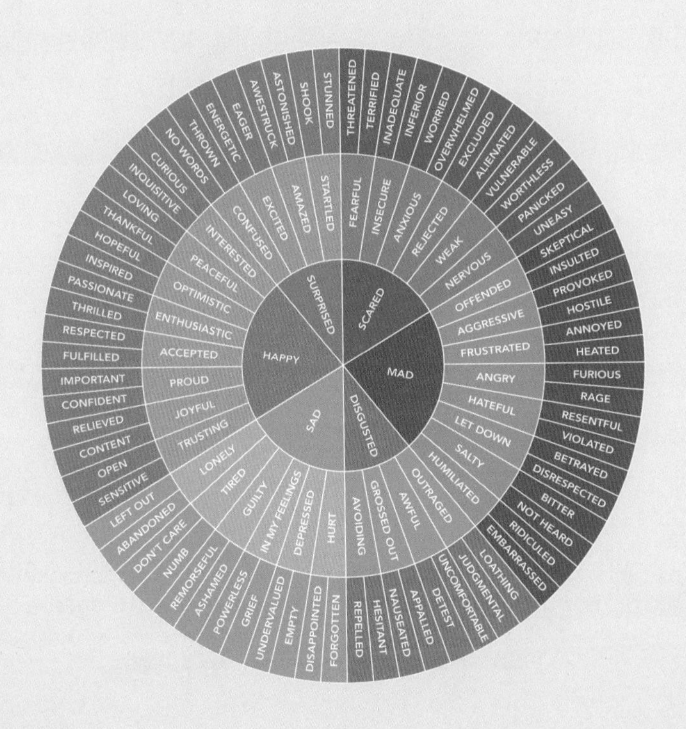

Say cheese! Don't forget to capture today.

Using the Feelings Wheel, write down 5 feelings you feel when change is happening.

Think about a big change you will face. Then, choose the main feeling you have when you think about change.

Fill in the blanks on the next page.

Everyday is a photo op.

Tear out this page and tape it to your mirror.

Even if I feel...

____

____

____

____

____

God you are bigger than...

____

____

____

____

____

Say cheese! Don't forget to capture today.

You can have courage even if...

Capture you at this moment.

// Hebrews 12:2a NLT

"We do this by keeping our eyes on Jesus, the champion who initiates and perfects our faith."

Do you want to win at life? Everyone does! The only issue is that there are so many opinions on what "winning" at life actually looks like. In reality, Jesus is the only example of what it means to be perfectly human. He is who we look to when we're looking for the best way to live–even in times of change. During his time on earth, He set a new way of life in motion through the way he acted, the things He taught, and how He treated other people. Now, we get to follow His example. When we "keep our eyes on Jesus" and focus on the way of life Jesus invites us into, the way we think about facing change is different. See, Jesus died and then came back to life three days later... and when that happens, you can assume that person knows how to truly live, despite what challenges or changes life brings.

Staying focused on Jesus helps me win at life because...

___

___

In my life, to win at facing change looks like...

___

___

___

___

___

You look good! You should take a picture or a video!

DAY 2

// Psalm 27:1 NLT

"The Lord is my light and my salvation—so why should I be afraid? The Lord is my fortress, protecting me from danger, so why should I tremble?"

We've all got stuff we are afraid of; it's normal: things like rejection, not measuring up, being alone, the negative opinions of others, the unknown, or sickness. Fear can be like a dark shadow over our lives–so powerful it almost feels like a prison. Feeling afraid is a human emotion. But we don't have to live trapped by fear. This Psalm reminds us what is true of God when our fear feels more true–what is real about God when our fear feels more real. In times when we're afraid, we can remember that God is bigger. God is our safe place.

Today, write out a prayer and say your fears out loud to God, and let His promises be light in your darkness.

Say cheese! Don't forget to capture today.

DAY 3

// Colossians 3:12 NIV

"Therefore, as God's chosen people, holy and dearly loved, clothe yourselves with compassion, kindness, humility, gentleness and patience."

What are you clothed with? Most of our thoughts automatically go to brands, styles, and trends... which makes perfect sense. Now, there are some more important things that we clothe ourselves with as well. Do you want to know what you're really clothed with? Think about your answer to this question: When other people see you, do they see things like compassion, humility, and patience? Your answer to this question reveals what your life and actions are clothed in. Is your life an example of the kinds of characteristics that show you are following Jesus?

Today, talk to the people who know you best like your friends, a small group leader, or parent–and ask them about what kind of characteristics they see when they look at you. If they see opportunities for you to grow in a specific area, ask them for advice on how to clothe yourself in more of that characteristic throughout your daily life.

I want to be clothed in:

___

The people around me see:

___

___

___

Capture you at this moment.

// James 1:5 NIV

"If any of you lacks wisdom, you should ask God, who gives generously to all without finding fault, and it will be given to you."

Do you ever feel stuck when you're trying to make decisions? Maybe you even seek advice, talk to people you trust, and spend a lot of time in deep thought. For whatever reason, you just can't get unstuck. Did you know that bringing these problems to God is the exact thing we should do? Not only that, God also wants to give you wisdom. The Creator of everything is the wisest One we can have access to. When you ask God for wisdom, God promises to give it to you generously.

Today, take some time to ask God to give you wisdom for the circumstances and situations where you need it most. List the names of people you trust to help you see God's wisdom in your life. Reach out to two of those people this week, and ask them to be praying for the specific areas where you desire wisdom.

Everyday is a photo op.

DAY 5

// Isaiah 41:10 ESV

"Fear not, for I am with you; be not dismayed, for I am your God; I will strengthen you, I will help you, I will uphold you with my righteous right hand."

There is no such thing as too much peace. We live in a time where anxiety, depression, and overwhelm run rampant. We have constant access to tragic news, bitter debates, and distracting content. This 24/7 stream of information is often more than we were designed to handle. We need something or Someone to bring us peace. Thankfully, this is what Jesus promised. When He could have promised power, money, and influence (things that seem like they would have been clutch nowadays), instead, He made peace the priority. He knows us better than we know ourselves. In our modern world, peace sounds so appealing.

Today, take a few minutes to write out a prayer, and ask God for peace. Then, be open to the fact that He may provide peace in ways that are different than you may be able to think of on your own.

Say cheese! Don't forget to capture today.

// John 16:33 NLT

"I have told you all this so that you may have peace in me. Here on earth you will have many trials and sorrows. But take heart, because I have overcome the world."

As much as we hate it, things change all the time. Everything changes, from small things like the weather to grades in school. Often, we don't worry about these changes. They can be frustrating at times, but they are things that will continue to change for better or worse. Other changes in our lives may include a loss of a family member or changes in friends. These changes can be harder to accept, but all these changes have one thing in common: God is with us in the middle of them. In the Bible, we are assured that God never changes. He is the same yesterday, today, and forever. There are days when our world feels like it is spinning and there is no way to stop it. It's like riding on a carousel or merry-go-round. The horses on the outside are continuously circling from the beginning of the ride to the end, but when from the middle of the ride, it remains still. While everything around it continues to spin, it remains stable. When we look to God, He is the only thing in our lives that remains unchanging. He offers us the courage and peace we need to get through changes and difficult situations because He is constantand has already overcome the world.

What are some things in your world that you would like for Jesus to overcome? Is it easy or difficult to believe that Jesus has overcome those things?

Capture you at this moment.

DAY 7: MEMORY VERSE

// Psalm 139:23 - 24 NIV

"Search me, God, and know my heart; test me and know my anxious thoughts. See if there is any offensive way in me, and lead me in the way everlasting."

Memorizing Scripture helps us align our perspective with God's perspective. This kind of thinking can transform the way we see society, other people, and ourselves. Committing Scripture to memory can help us begin to see life through the lens of what God says is true.

1. Create flashcards with each word of today's Scripture.

2. Ask a friend or someone at home to review the flash cards every morning this week.

3. At the end of each day, try to write down the Scripture from memory and pay attention to your progress throughout the week.

Don't forget to capture a picture or a video clip of yourself today.

PART 4

GOD CAN USE CHANGE TO MAKE YOU STRONGER

One thing I want to change is...

Jot down a list of things you want to change for the better.
Then choose one to focus on and write it in the circle.

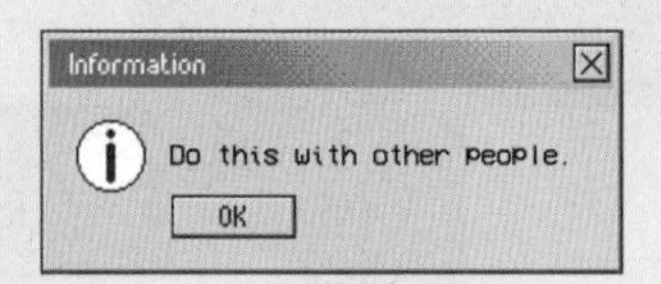

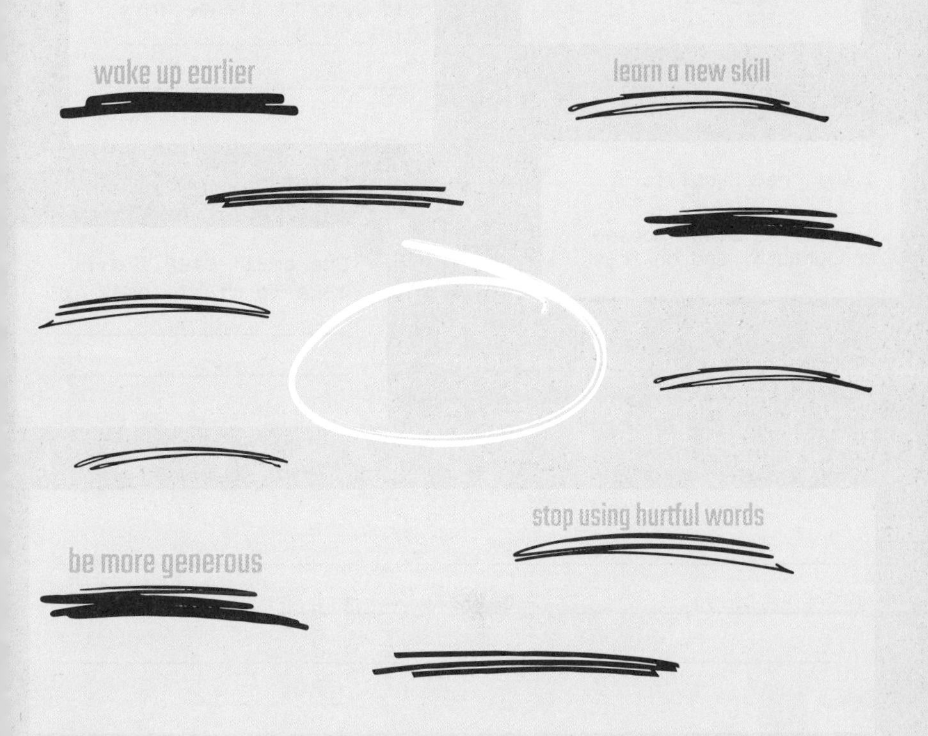

You look good! You should take a picture or a video!

I want to change this because...

I want to change
this because
____
____________________.

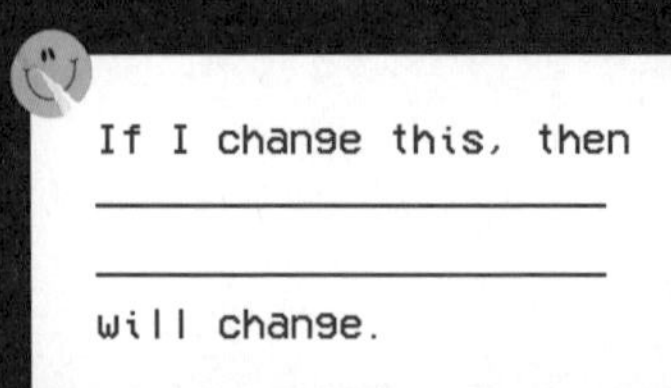
If I change this, then
____
____
will change.

If I don't change this,
then ____________________
____________________.

I will reach out to
____
to help me stay focused,
encouraged, and on track.

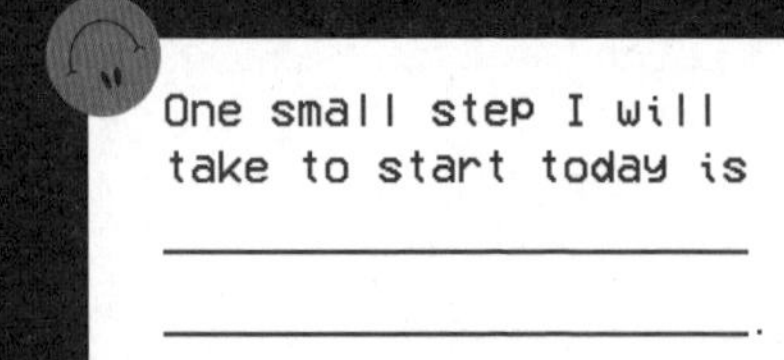
One small step I will
take to start today is
____
____________________.

Here is my plan for working
toward my change goal over
the next few weeks 👇

____
____
____

You look good! You should take a picture or a video!

What could keep me from making this change?

What will I do to overcome the obstacles
I may face on my way to change?

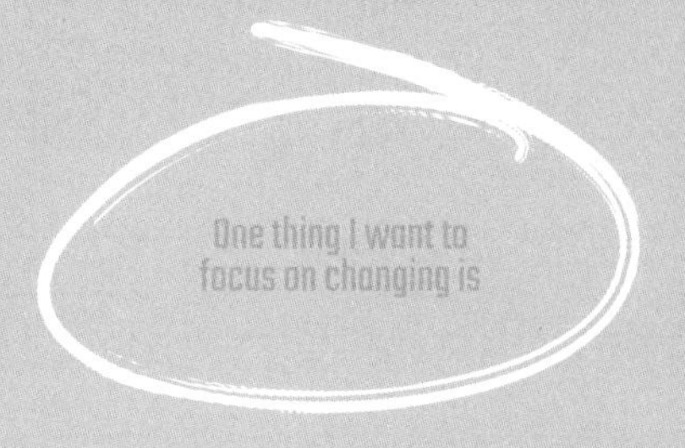

Say cheese! Don't forget to capture today.

God can use change to make you stronger even if...

It's true that God can use change to make you stronger, even if it's a change you don't want to go through. What are ways change makes us stronger?

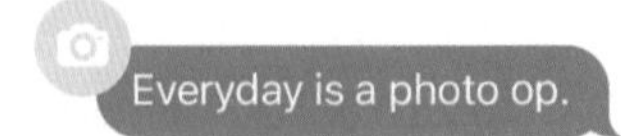

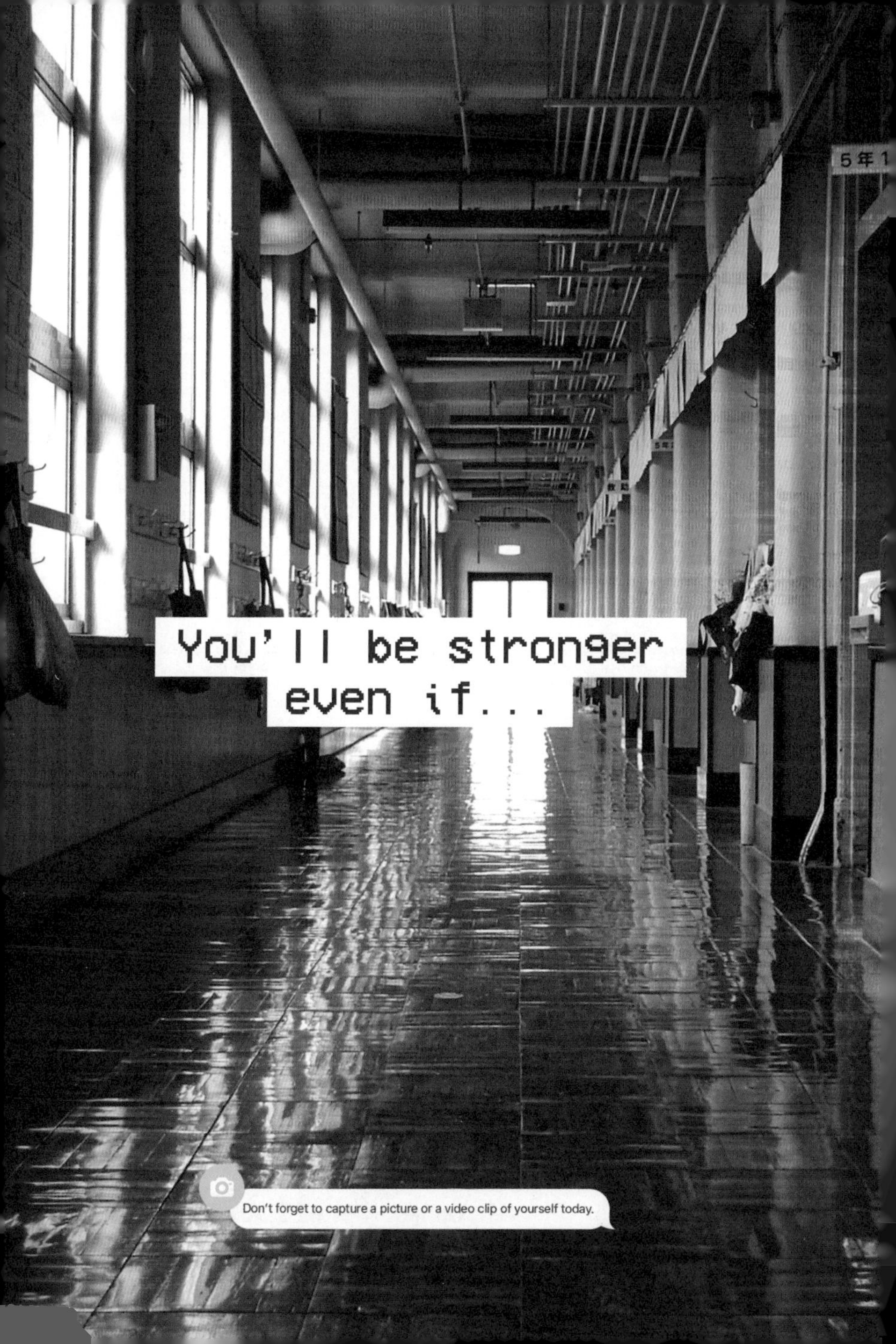

You'll be stronger
even if...

Don't forget to capture a picture or a video clip of yourself today.

DAY 1

// Romans 12:2 NLT

"Don't copy the behavior and customs of this world, but let God transform you into a new person by changing the way you think. Then you will learn to know God's will for you, which is good and pleasing and perfect."

Have you seen something in nature completely transform? Think about a caterpillar turning into a butterfly or a tadpole turning into a frog. It's pretty incredible to think God is also in the business of transforming us. But instead of an outward change, today's verse tells us God is most interested in transforming our inward being—our thoughts. God wants us to focus on changing our minds and what we think about it. Why? Because what we think about not only impacts what we say and do but impacts the way we love God, love others, and love life.

On the left, write down a thought you want to change. Then, on the right, write down what you want to change it to.

Ex. I am afraid to make the wrong decision about something big I am facing.	Ex. I am confident that my future is secure in God.

Say cheese! Don't forget to capture today.

DAY 2

// Proverbs 3:5 NLT

"Trust in the Lord with all your heart; do not depend on your own understanding."

Has there ever been a time in your life when you were so certain things were one way, only to find out that wasn't the entire story? Maybe you thought your stepmom was terrible–until you really got to know her. Or maybe you thought switching schools was a bad idea–until you realized you like your new school more. It's easy to rush to judgment before we have the entire picture. In those moments of uncertainty, God invites us to lean into His perspective. In other words, He invites us to trust His understanding of the situation and His knowledge of the big picture.

Sometimes the most challenging part of facing change is wanting to know what will happen in the future. We want to have more control than our present circumstances allow. Write out a prayer to God that you can come back and read to remind yourself that you can trust God....

____

____

____

____

____

____

____

You look good! You should take a picture or a video!

DAY 3

// Ecclesiastes 3:1 NLT

"For everything there is a season, a time for every activity under heaven."

Do you have a favorite season of the year? Maybe it's one of the four seasons, such as spring or fall. Or maybe your preferred season revolves around a certain sport or activity, like basketball or soccer. No matter what your favorite time of year is, God has designated every activity—every unique season in our lives—for a certain time. And once that season is finished, it's time for another to take its place. Instead of being frustrated about a particular season coming to an end in your life, pray and ask God to remind you that each season brings new challenges and new experiences—and the opportunity for new-found joy and excitement along the way.

Reflect on how you feel about the seasons of your life changing from one to the next. Knowing that change is unavoidable, how can you prepare to lean in and trust God in the process?

Say cheese! Don't forget to capture today.

// Colossians 3:2 NLT

"Think about the things of heaven, not the things of earth."

What consumes your thoughts? Is it the stress of homework? The pressure of figuring out how to connect with your crush? The replay of what you didn't do in your last game? Our thoughts are loud and they take up a lot more time than we typically realize. So, what would it look like for you to set your thoughts on "the things of heaven?" This doesn't mean you have to think about spiritual things constantly. However, it does mean that you bring spiritual perspective into your ordinary thoughts. Maybe you think about what it would look like to treat your crush like God says is best. Maybe you think about the way you use your influence on the field to point your friends to Jesus. Maybe you think about why you're doing homework, not just for yourself, but out of respect for the leaders (teachers) in your life. Bringing a spiritual perspective to your thoughts may sound a little out there, but with the amount of time you spend thinking, this could change everything.

Today, write down a few of the most consistent thoughts you've had lately. Then rewrite those thoughts with a "things of heaven" perspective.

____

____

____

____

____

____

Everyday is a photo op.

// Romans 5:3 NLT

"We can rejoice, too, when we run into problems and trials, for we know that they help us develop endurance."

Nothing about our problems feels exciting. Life would be so much easier if we didn't have to go through difficult moments. However, Paul, the author of Romans says that our problems can actually push us to joy. Here's how: Overcoming challenges builds endurance. It's just like exercise. In the moment, our bodies are pushed to their limits, but we know that the resistance makes us stronger. God can use your challenging circumstances to do the same thing in your life.

Find three trusted adults and ask them, "How has God used problems and trials to build endurance in your life?" Take notes on their responses below:

____

____

____

____

____

____

____

Say cheese! Don't forget to capture today.

// Proverbs 3:5-6 NLT

"Trust in the Lord with all your heart; do not depend on your own understanding. Seek his will in all you do, and he will show you which path to take."

Change can be hard. In this world, we see change all the time, and some of that change is not comfortable or enjoyable. It disturbs our life and can make things really difficult. The future can be a very uncertain thing that we as teens tend to stress about. It feels like this big, looming shadow that you can't escape. I had a big fear of the future at one point. Thinking about it was scary; it felt so uncertain. Then I realized that as a child of God, I had no reason to fear the future. As this verse says, as long as we seek God in all we do, He will show us where to go in life. We may not always see where He is going and may want to become a backseat driver, but we need to trust that He knows best, because He does. He's God. He knows all and is always good, even when life is not. So even when we don't understand where on Earth He is taking us, we can be sure that as long as we're following Him, He will never steer us wrong.

When we depend on our own understanding of a situation we are facing, we are limited. How would your life be different if you put more focus on God's perspective than your own? What is challenging about that?

____

____

____

____

____

____

You look good! You should take a picture or a video!

DAY 7: MEMORY VERSE

// Philippians 4:6-7 NIV

6 "Do not be anxious about anything, but in every situation, by prayer and petition, with thanksgiving, present your requests to God."
7 "And the peace of God, which transcends all understanding, will guard your hearts and your minds in Christ Jesus."

When we memorize Scripture, we are able to recall what's really true in a world full of so many different opinions. We're bombarded with all sorts of facts and opinions each and every day. This overwhelming amount of information can confuse and distract us from what's true and best. Memorizing Scripture helps us to focus on the truth when we need it most.

1. When you set your wake-up alarm this week, add the text of Philippians 4:6-7 to it.

2. Each morning, when your alarm goes off, start your day by reading the Scripture; then delete the text from your alarm.

3. Then, every night before bed, rewrite the Scripture from memory in a new alarm for the next morning.

____

____

____

____

____

____

____

Don't forget to capture a picture or a video clip of yourself today.

Think of something you are worried or excited about in the future.

FILL IN THE BLANK

Even if ________________________________ just remember,

GOD NEVER CHANGES.

GOD IS WITH YOU.

GOD IS BIGGER THAN YOUR FEAR.

GOD CAN USE CHANGE TO MAKE YOU STRONGER.

Check out the playlist "Even If - Change Journal" to help you face life's biggest changes.

Don't forget to post pages from your change journal or your 30 Day Photo Challenge using #EvenIfJournal

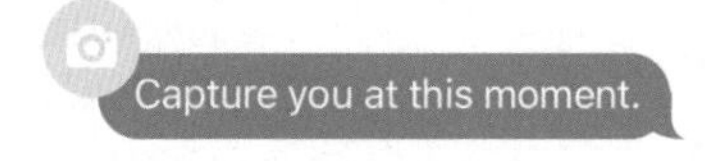